My World of Science

HOT AND COLD

Angela Royston

Heinemann
LIBRARY

www.heinemann.co.uk/library
Visit our website to find out more information about **Heinemann Library** books.

To order:
 Phone 44 (0) 1865 888066
Send a fax to 44 (0) 1865 314091
 Visit the Heinemann Bookshop at www.heinemann.co.uk/library to browse our catalogue and order online.

First published in Great Britain by Heinemann Library, Halley Court, Jordan Hill, Oxford, OX2 8EJ, a division of Reed Educational & Professional Publishing Ltd. Heinemann is a registered trademark of Reed Educational & Professional Publishing Ltd.

OXFORD   MELBOURNE   AUCKLAND   JOHANNESBURG   BLANTYRE
GABORONE   IBADAN   PORTSMOUTH NH (USA)   CHICAGO

Designed by bigtop, Bicester, UK
Originated by Ambassador Litho Ltd.
Printed and bound in Hong Kong/China

06 05 04 03 02   06 05 04 03 02
10 9 8 7 6 5 4 3 2   10 9 8 7 6 5 4 3 2 1

ISBN 0 431 13715 3 (hardback)   ISBN 0 431 13721 8 (paperback)

British Library Cataloguing in Publication Data
Royston, Angela
Hot and cold. – (My world of science)
1. Temperature – Juvenile literature 2. Cold – Juvenile literature
3. Heat – Juvenile literature I. Title
536.5

Acknowledgements
The Publishers would like to thank the following for permission to reproduce photographs:
Eye Ubiquitous: Sylvia Greenland p7; Robert Harding: pp4, 8; Science Photo Library: p14, Ricardo Arias, Latin Stock p22, Geoff Tompkinson p9; Stone: p5; Trevor Clifford: pp6, 10, 11, 12, 13, 15, 16, 17, 19, 20, 21, 23, 24, 25, 26, 27, 28, 29; Trip: H Rogers p18.

Cover photograph reproduced with permission of Images.

Every effort has been made to contact copyright holders of any material reproduced in this book. Any omissions will be rectified in subsequent printings if notice is given to the Publisher.

Contents

Any words appearing in the text in bold, **like this**, are explained in the Glossary.

Hot and cold

Some things are hot. This jacket potato is hot. When food is very hot, you can see **steam** rising from it. Be careful not to burn your mouth.

Some things are cold. Ice cream is very cold. As you lick the ice cream, it makes your lips and tongue cold too.

Danger!

Many things may be so hot they can burn and hurt you. A cooker may be very hot. What else in the picture will be very hot too?

Keep away from hot things even when they are turned off. A hot iron smoothes out creases in clothes. It stays hot for a long time after it has been turned off.

Neither hot nor cold

Some things are neither hot nor cold.
The water in a swimming pool is said
to be cool, warm or **lukewarm**.

This baby's bathwater is warmer than the water in a swimming pool. But it is cooler than your bathwater.

Temperature

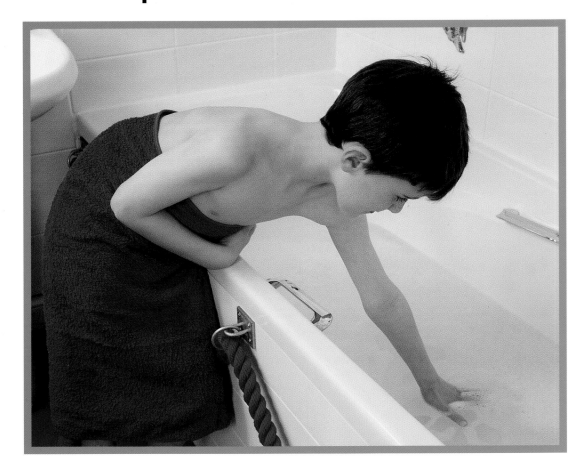

We use words like warm, cool, hot and cold to talk about **temperature**. The boy is testing the temperature of the bathwater with his hand.

Different parts of the body feel
temperature differently. The
bathwater will probably feel hotter
to the boy's foot than to his hand.

Testing temperatures

| warm water | cold water |

Temperatures can feel different when you are hot or cold. The girl is holding her hands in warm water. The boy is holding his in cold water.

lukewarm water

Now they both put their hands in **lukewarm** water. The girl says it feels cool. The boy says it feels warm.

Thermometers

A **thermometer measures temperature** exactly. This doctor is using a thermometer to measure the temperature of the girl's body.

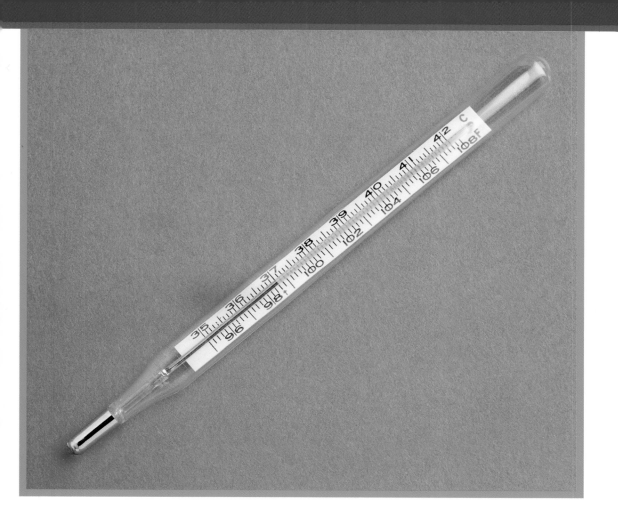

The end of the silver line shows the temperature. This person's temperature is normal at 37 °C. When you are ill, your temperature can get hotter.

More thermometers

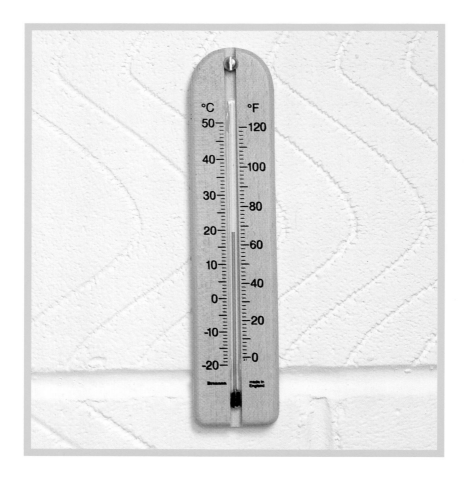

This **thermometer measures** the **temperature** of the air in a room. It shows 20 °C. The room will be nice and warm.

This thermometer measures the
temperature of the air outside.
A temperature of 30 °C is very hot.
But 5 °C is very cold.

Keeping cool

In hot weather we dress to keep ourselves as cool as possible. Many people wear light, loose clothes. These protect them from the Sun.

Wind can make you feel cooler. This girl is holding a fan which makes a wind. The wind cools her down.

Keeping warm

In cold weather we need to keep warm. What special clothes are these children putting on to keep warm?

Insulation keeps warm air in and cold air out. This window has two layers of glass to keep the heat in. Curtains help to insulate the house as well.

Cooking

Food is cooked by making it hot. Some food, like this meat, must be cooked to make it safe to eat.

This girl is making a cake. She stirs the **ingredients** to make a sloppy mixture. When the mixture is cooked in a hot oven, it turns solid.

Fridges

A fridge keeps food colder than the air in the room does. When food is stored in a cold fridge, it stays **fresh** for longer.

The bottom of the fridge is the coldest part. But if there is a freezer **compartment**, it is even colder. What is stored in the coldest part of this fridge?

Freezing

A freezer keeps food even colder than a fridge. Some frozen food will keep for two or three months. Things get hard and cold when they freeze.

This boy is putting a tray of water into the freezer. The water will get colder. When it reaches 0 °C, it will turn into solid ice cubes.

Melting

This boy is enjoying an ice cream. As the cold ice cream becomes warmer, it starts to melt. It changes from solid spoonfuls into a runny liquid.

If you heat chocolate, it will start to
melt. When the chocolate cools down,
it becomes solid again.

Glossary

compartment small box

fresh nice to eat, not old

ingredients the different parts of a mixture

insulation a material that keeps heat in and cold out

lukewarm slightly warm

measure to find out how big, heavy, hot or cold something is

steam tiny droplets of very hot water that float in the air

temperature how hot or cold something is

thermometer something that measures temperature

Answers

Page 6 – Danger!
The roasting tin and the saucepan will be very hot too.

Page 20 – Keeping warm
The children are putting on coats, hats, scarves, gloves and heavy shoes to keep warm.

Page 25 – Fridges
Vegetables, milk and juice are stored in the coldest part of the fridge.

Index